W9-CCF-405

George C. Marshall

History Maker Bios

Catherine A. Welch

LERNER PUBLICATIONS COMPANY • MINNEAPOLIS

To slow learners and late bloomers—get excited about something, believe in yourself, and do your best!

The author thanks Michael Welch, William Welch, Valerie Oakley, Raymond Bouley, Judith Stark, Dawn Higginson, and the staff of the Southbury, CT, Public Library for help in gathering material for this book.

Illustrations by Tim Parlin

Text copyright © 2005 by Catherine A. Welch
Illustrations copyright © 2005 by Lerner Publications Company

All rights reserved. International copyright secured. No part of this book may be reproduced, stored in a retrieval system, or transmitted in any form or by any means—electronic, mechanical, photocopying, recording, or otherwise—without the prior written permission of Lerner Publications Company, except for the inclusion of brief quotations in an acknowledged review.

Lerner Publications Company
A division of Lerner Publishing Group
241 First Avenue North
Minneapolis, MN 55401 U.S.A.

Website address: www.lernerbooks.com

Library of Congress Cataloging-in-Publication Data

Welch, Catherine A.
    George C. Marshall / By Catherine A. Welch.
      p.   cm. — (History maker bios)
    Includes bibliographical references and index.
    ISBN: 0–8225–2435–X (lib. bdg. : alk. paper)
      1. Marshall, George C. (George Catlett), 1880–1959—Juvenile literature.
    2. Generals—United States—Biography—Juvenile literature. 3. United States.
    Army—Biography—Juvenile literature. 4. United States—History, Military—
    20th century—Juvenile literature. I. Title. II. Series.
    E745.M37W45 2005
    973.918′092—dc22   2004002594

Manufactured in the United States of America
1 2 3 4 5 6 – JR – 10 09 08 07 06 05

TABLE OF CONTENTS

INTRODUCTION

George Catlett Marshall was born on December 31, 1880, fifteen years after the Civil War ended. He became a soldier during peaceful times, when the United States had only a small army. But in the 1900s, two world wars changed everything.

Marshall worked to build a large, well-trained and equipped military. He helped the United States become a new world superpower. And when the wars were over, this man who had helped his country prepare for war began working for peace.

This is his story.

A SLOW LEARNER

George Marshall was born in Uniontown, Pennsylvania. As a child, he was a slow learner. He had trouble with math, grammar, and spelling. His classmates laughed at him. His older sister Marie called him the "dunce of the class."

The laughter hurt George. He sometimes used pranks to get even. One night, he put a frog in Marie's bed. Other times, he dropped water bombs on her boyfriends.

At times, George's father beat him for these pranks. George Marshall Sr. kept a willow stick in the basement. But he never beat Marie or George's older brother, Stuart.

George's mother did not like to see him beaten. Laura Bradford Marshall loved her son. She could even laugh at his pranks. She tried to hide George's pranks from her husband.

George (RIGHT) with his brother Stuart (CENTER) and his sister Marie (LEFT) in 1884

George did share a few good times with his father. They went hunting and fishing together. On one trip, George and his father caught thirty bass.

George's father spoke often of the smart, famous Marshalls of the past. In 1801, John Marshall was named chief justice of the U.S. Supreme Court. George's great-grandfather and John Marshall were first cousins.

George felt he could never be a smart Marshall. He thought his father was ashamed of him. By the time George was nine years old, he gave up trying to learn.

CHILDHOOD CHORES

George grew up next to the Coal Lick Creek. Horse-drawn streetcars passed in front of the Marshall's redbrick house. George had the chore of hosing down the horse droppings. He also had a weekly chore at Saint Peter's Episcopal Church. Using bellows, he pumped air for the organ.

The Marshall home in Uniontown, Pennsylvania

George and his friend Andy Thompson built a place to grow plants in a shed behind the Marshalls' house. They grew tomatoes and sold them to the local grocer.

One summer, the boys made a waterway along the creek. They built a fleet of small ships. They pretended it was the U.S. Navy.

George often thought about past battles. Local statues and gravestones reminded him of war. His father also told him tales of Pennsylvania's history.

Young George loved history. He liked reading about Benjamin Franklin and the

Confederate general Robert E. Lee. He also liked reading about Bluebeard the pirate. One book stated that a Marshall woman may have married Bluebeard.

General Robert E. Lee led the Confederate army during the Civil War.

When he was sixteen, George thought about joining the U.S. Army. He wanted to enter the Virginia Military Institute. Stuart had graduated from this military college in 1894.

But Stuart did not want his brother to enter the institute. One day, George overheard Stuart arguing with their mother. Stuart said George would disgrace the family.

Stuart's words lit a fire in George. How dare Stuart say that! George wanted to prove his brother wrong. He would work hard. He would never give up again. It was time a *new* Marshall made a mark in history!

2 DYNAMITE MARSHALL

Before George entered the Virginia Military Institute, he was sick with typhoid fever. He was weak and pale when he started school.

The students at the military school were called cadets. The senior cadets made life hard for new cadets. George struggled through drills and exercises. He scrubbed toilets. He ran errands for the seniors. When things got tough, he thought of Stuart's words. He would *not* disgrace the family.

Soon George Marshall stood out as a leader. By the time he graduated, he was in charge of the cadets at all the ceremonies. He had a full, strong voice. It seemed to echo when he shouted a command.

During this time, he met Elizabeth Carter Coles, known as Lily. After he graduated from the institute, the couple married. A week later, Marshall reported for duty in the Philippines, islands then under U.S. control. He was a second lieutenant in the U.S. Army.

George Marshall (FRONT RIGHT) in 1901 as a cadet at the Virginia Military Institute

13

The U.S. military was in the Philippines to keep peace on the islands. This was not a full-scale war. On the island of Mindoro, Marshall led jungle patrols in crocodile-filled streams. The senior officers were impressed with him. At the age of 22, he was already calm and in control.

He often thought about Lily. He missed his wife. She had a heart condition and could not often travel with him.

During peacetime, Marshall had no chance of leading troops on the battlefield. He had little chance to earn a higher position in the army. By 1914, Marshall had served for twelve years. He felt like leaving the army.

Marshall (FRONT ROW, CENTER) with his infantry group in the Philippines in 1903

A Peacetime Army

In 1890, the U.S. Army was small. It had twenty-five thousand trained men. Many Americans did not see a need for a large military force. They felt the oceans would keep the country safe from most attacks. They also believed that volunteers could be quickly called to fight during wartime.

Then World War I started in Europe, with Germany fighting France, Great Britain, and Russia. George stayed in the army. The United States might enter that war. He saw a chance to lead troops.

By 1916, France and Great Britain urged President Woodrow Wilson to send troops to Europe. They asked the United States to join them as allies, or partners, in the war. The United States had to act fast. The army needed more men and weapons.

Marshall became a captain. His job was to help General James Franklin Bell train men in the California military program.

The men were volunteers and had paid for their own uniforms and equipment. Many of the men had powerful friends in politics. Bell warned Marshall that these men might not like harsh treatment. If Marshall was too hard on them, he could lose his chance to move up in the army.

But Marshall did his job. He drilled the men so hard that they nicknamed him Dynamite Marshall. But the men respected him.

Soldiers practice climbing over a wall as part of their military training.

German submarines (FRONT) sank many merchant ships (BACK) and passenger ships during World War I.

In 1917, German submarines sank many U.S. ships. On April 6, the United States declared war on Germany. General John J. Pershing was chosen to lead the U.S. forces in France. Marshall hoped to go with Pershing.

But he got a different job. He was ordered to help General William L. Sibert form the U.S. 1st Infantry Division in France. Marshall became a temporary lieutenant colonel. His job was to check conditions on the battlefield.

Life in the narrow trenches was difficult.

In France, U.S. troops trained and fought in trenches. Heavy rain caused the trenches to fill with water. Marshall trudged through mud under the cover of fog. He dodged gunfire and explosions. He always carried a gas mask in case the Germans attacked with poison gas. This was his greatest fear.

The troops suffered in muddy trenches that were filled with rats. They ate meals outdoors, often in snow. They were tired and cold. They needed firewood, blankets, clothing, and food. Even the horses were starving. They were eating their leather and rope halter straps.

Marshall reported his findings to headquarters. He worked hard to get supplies. But the army had no way to get the supplies to the troops quickly. The men continued to suffer.

During the war, Marshall admired General Pershing's work. U.S. troops were not trained for the hardships and horrors of war. But Pershing promised to make U.S. troops the best soldiers in the world.

Pershing was also impressed with Marshall. During the war, Marshall took on the job of quickly moving 500,000 troops for a major battle. The troops first fought a battle at Saint-Mihiel, France. Then they marched sixty miles, secretly at night, to the Meuse-Argonne battlefront. They moved field kitchens, hospitals, and more than 2,700 guns over rough roads.

3 BETWEEN WORLD WARS

World War I ended in 1918. By then, millions of people in Europe had suffered and died. In Paris, France, Marshall saw crowds weep during victory parades. France and its allies had won. But everyone had lost someone in the war. Marshall looked at the faces of these people. He would never forget the sorrow he saw that day.

In 1921, Pershing became chief of staff of the U.S. Army. He was in charge of planning for the entire army. Marshall was Pershing's aide. He prepared reports for Congress about the country's defense. He wrote Pershing's speeches. Sometimes he even *gave* the speeches. He did most of Pershing's job, but never complained.

During this time, George and Lily were together. He wanted a family, but they never had children. He did have a goddaughter, Rose Page. Her father was a professor at the University of Virginia. Marshall bought Rose a pony and taught her how to ride it. Marshall and Lily treated Rose like their own daughter.

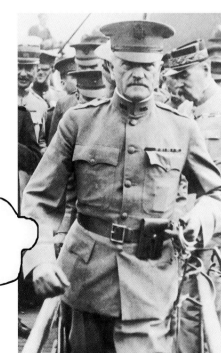

Marshall worked closely with General John J. Pershing.

In 1927, Marshall started teaching at the Army War College in Washington, D.C. Then Lily died suddenly. Marshall could not bear losing Lily. He lost so much weight that his doctor gave him a warning. If his health got worse, he could be kicked out of the army.

When Marshall heard that, he snapped out of his grief. Soon after, he got a job at Fort Benning, Georgia. He missed Lily, but his job at the Army Infantry School was a dream come true.

George and Lily Marshall (LEFT) had been married for twenty-five years when Lily passed away in 1927.

Soldiers train on the grounds of Fort Benning in the 1930s.

Fort Benning was the U.S. Army's largest military training school. The training grounds had forests, streams, and rolling hills. It was the perfect place to practice for war.

Marshall knew the conditions of a real battlefield. Things keep changing on a battlefield. Tanks can suddenly appear from behind clouds of smoke. At night, troops cannot see what is happening. The battlefield is a confusing place.

At Fort Benning in the early 1930s, soldiers train in preparation for real battles.

Marshall turned Fort Benning's grounds into practice battlefields with tanks, smoke-laying planes, and artillery. His students often trained at night. At times, Marshall didn't give them maps of the grounds.

These students would be officers someday. They must lead their troops to victory and safety. Marshall forced the students to plan their next battlefield moves quickly. He kept a small black book with names of the best students.

In 1929, he met Katherine Tupper Brown. Katherine was a widow who had two sons, Clifton and Allen, and a daughter Molly. In 1930, George and Katherine married.

By 1932, the United States was in an economic depression. Businesses were failing. People lost jobs. In cities, hungry crowds stood in mile-long lines to get food.

Congress wanted to cut the number of army officers from twelve thousand to ten thousand. Soon, there were not many jobs for full colonels like Marshall.

TEACHING BY EXAMPLE

George Marshall felt that setting a good example often worked better than giving orders. After marrying Katherine, he got a new job at Fort Screven, Georgia. The place was run-down, and the soldiers' spirits were low. George and Katherine quickly spruced up their yard with shrubs, flowers, and a vegetable plot. The younger officers saw this and did the same.

President Franklin D. Roosevelt asked Congress to support the idea of a Civilian Conservation Corps (CCC). The CCC gave thousands of young men a chance to work. CCC camps were set up around the country. The army took charge of these camps.

Marshall took charge of a camp near Charleston, South Carolina. The young men who came were poor and sick. Some had rotting teeth, skin sores, and rashes. Many men could not read or write. Many officers did not like the job of helping these men. But Marshall did.

A CCC poster offers jobs to young men.

Marshall brought in dentists to clean their teeth. He gave lessons in reading and writing. The men began smiling with pride. The army had the men clean streams and beaches and repair roads and bridges.

By 1938, Germany was about to attack France and Great Britain. Marshall became assistant chief of staff of the army. He believed the United States should prepare for another world war.

But Roosevelt had different ideas. Most Americans did not want to enter another war. They wanted to let Great Britain and France fight Germany alone.

The president wanted to help. But he also wanted to please Americans and get reelected. Marshall understood this. He knew he must learn how to work in Washington, D.C. He must learn about politics.

4 WORLD WAR II

In 1939, Europe was at war again. There was also fighting in Asia. Japan had attacked China. That year, Marshall became a general and chief of staff of the army. He told the president and Congress to prepare for war. The U.S. Army had fewer than 200,000 men.

Marshall wanted a military that could move quickly. It needed 1,000 ships to move 5 million men and supplies to Europe. It needed more than 2 million jeeps and trucks. It needed more than 80,000 tanks, 120,000 combat planes, 12 million rifles, and 2 million machine guns.

Marshall also wanted to lower the draft age to eighteen. Many people disliked this idea. But Marshall knew that a soldier needed strong legs for marching and a strong body for sleepless days on the battlefield. He wanted millions of young men trained.

Tanks line up to be loaded onto ships and carried across the ocean for use in World War II.

He also wanted young officers to replace older officers. Marshall, already sixty years old himself, planned to retire as soon as the younger officers were in place. But President Roosevelt would not let him retire.

In a radio address, Marshall warned the public that time was running out. Meanwhile, his stepsons, Allen and Clifton, joined the military.

In 1940, Congress passed a bill giving $9 billion to the army. Americans still did not understand that the country could be attacked soon. But Marshall saw the danger.

Marshall's stepsons, Allen (LEFT) and Clifton, both joined the military during World War II.

The military used a machine like this one to decode secret messages.

In Washington, D.C., the military had four machines that could pick up Japan's secret military messages. Marshall knew that Japan might attack the U.S. naval base in Pearl Harbor, Hawaii. He put all military forces there on alert.

By fall of 1941, attention turned to the Philippines. But the military kept decoding Japanese messages. Marshall felt the commanders in Hawaii were still on alert.

The day after the attack on Pearl Harbor, the United States entered World War II.

Decoding the Japanese messages took time. Somehow, the system failed. On December 7, 1941, the Japanese launched a surprise attack on Pearl Harbor. On December 8, the United States and Great Britain declared war on Japan. Three days later, Germany and Italy declared war on the United States.

Suddenly, the Unites States was in a worldwide war. When choosing officers, Marshall went to his black book of names. Two names were Dwight D. Eisenhower and George S. Patton. Marshall chose well. These men became two of the most important generals in the war.

Soon Marshall had three thousand officers and men reporting to him. Each hour, he got updates about the war. And he tried to keep up with what President Roosevelt and Congress were thinking.

Millions of people were counting on Marshall. He took daily walks to keep healthy. He tried not to get angry. Anger would drain his energy. "My brain must be kept clear," he said.

Marshall enjoyed horseback riding for exercise and relaxation. His dog Fleet joins him for the ride.

Each week, he gave Roosevelt a list of those wounded or killed. He often wrote notes to the parents and wives of soldiers who died. His own stepson Allen was killed. Marshall was heartbroken but had no time to stop to grieve.

Marshall worried about the spirits of the troops. He flew more than a million miles to military stations. He listened to the men's complaints. He sent chaplains to battlefronts to pray with the troops. "The soldier's heart, the soldier's spirit, the soldier's soul, are everything," he said.

LIFTING SPIRITS

Weary troops were often homesick. They feared being wounded or killed. Marshall looked for ways to lift their spirits. The men needed reminders of home. Ice cream and fresh bread sometimes helped. Hollywood stars, such as Bob Hope, entertained troops, bringing laughter and songs. But most of all, the soldiers wanted mail from home.

Marshall (LEFT) stands by as President Roosevelt (CENTER) and Winston Churchill (RIGHT) have a conversation.

Marshall longed to be the supreme commander, leading Allied troops in Europe. But Roosevelt needed him in Washington, D.C., to make war plans. Marshall also went to meetings with world leaders, including Winston Churchill, the British prime minister.

Things continued to change at home. On December 17, 1944, Marshall became a five-star general of the army, the highest rank for an officer. On April 12, 1945, President Roosevelt died. Harry S. Truman became president.

On May 9, 1945, Germany surrendered. But it looked like Japan would never surrender. Truman turned to Marshall and Secretary of War Henry Stimson for advice.

A war in Japan would be long. Many U.S. soldiers would die. Marshall and Stimson wanted to end the war. They decided the fastest way to end the war was to use a new weapon called the atomic bomb on Japan.

On August 6, 1945, a U.S. plane dropped an atomic bomb on the Japanese city of Hiroshima. Still, Japan did not surrender. Three days later, the United States dropped an atomic bomb on the city of Nagasaki. Japan soon surrendered.

About fifty million people died during World War II. More than eight million young Americans had been trained for war. Marshall was sad. The world had changed forever.

5 WORLD POWER AND PEACE

Marshall's duty as chief of staff ended in November 1945. He was almost sixty-five. He planned winter trips to Florida. He also wanted to spend time at a cabin in Pinehurst, North Carolina.

But President Truman had other plans for Marshall. Marshall's wife was furious. She wanted her husband to retire. But Marshall felt he had a duty to serve his country.

Marhall (CENTER) worked with Chinese leaders to try to find a solution for the Chinese civil war.

His next job was to help end the civil war in China. The United States hoped the two sides, the Communists and the Nationalists, could share power in China.

Marshall worked hard to understand Chinese politics. He tried to please both the Communists and Nationalists. He almost got both sides to work together. But it seemed that nobody trusted him. Marshall failed and blamed himself.

During this time, the United States looked back at the attack on Pearl Harbor. People wondered who should be blamed.

Republicans in Congress wanted to prove that Roosevelt, a Democrat, led the nation into war. Marshall spent six days in Congress answering questions about the Pearl Harbor attack. Marshall explained that the days before the war had been hectic. Everyone had done their best to decode the Japanese messages and get warnings out quickly.

Marshall continued to serve his country. On January 21, 1947, he became secretary of state. His job was to help the president and the United States deal with foreign countries.

Marshall (LEFT) is sworn in as secretary of state.

At this time, Europe was still struggling to recover from war. The winter of 1947 was bitterly cold. Food was scarce. People were starving and dying.

Millions of skilled workers had died during the war. Railroads, highways, and ports were destroyed. So were coal mines and steel mines. The land was no longer in shape for farming. Many of the cows, pigs, and sheep were gone.

The only countries strong enough to help Europe were the United States and the Soviet Union, the country formerly known as Russia. These countries had been allies during the war. But now they did not trust each other.

The bombing during World War II left much of Berlin, Germany, in ruins by 1945.

Marshall did not seek fame. But he became famous. Some wanted him to run for president in 1944. Marshall didn't want that kind of attention. But sometimes he needed support for his ideas. His picture was often taken with important people. He used the newspapers and radio to spread his ideas about a plan to rebuild Europe.

The Soviet Union did not want Americans to expand their businesses into Europe. The United States did not want the Soviet Union to take control of the governments in the weak European countries.

On June 5, 1947, Marshall gave a speech at Harvard University. He spoke of the suffering in Europe. In his speech, Marshall said that a plan to rebuild Europe must come *from* Europe. The nations of Europe must work together with the United States' help.

Marshall worked hard to get support from Congress and the American people. The plan became known as the Marshall Plan.

Congress finally agreed to give billions of dollars to help Europe. Immediately, the United States sent nineteen thousand tons of wheat to Europe. Soon after, hundreds of ships were crossing the Atlantic with cotton, tires, tractors, chemicals, oil, and horsemeat.

Workers unload bags of wheat in the Netherlands as part of the Marshall Plan.

Marshall was sixty-eight when his duty as secretary of state ended. President Truman quickly named him president of the American Red Cross. The Red Cross helps people after disasters, such as floods, earthquakes, and hurricanes.

In June 1950, North Korea attacked South Korea. Marshall became the U.S. secretary of defense and helped the country respond to the war. He retired in 1951. In 1953, Marshall received the Nobel Peace Prize for his work helping Europe after World War II.

Soon after, his health began to fail. He was ill with colds and bronchitis. He fell and cracked a rib. He later suffered two strokes. Marshall died on October 16, 1959.

As a young boy, he never dreamed he would be a great Marshall. He never dreamed he would be a world leader. But George C. Marshall is forever a part of history because one day, he decided to try his best. He decided he would *never* stop trying.

TIMELINE

GEORGE C. MARSHALL
WAS BORN ON
DECEMBER 31, 1880.

In the year . . .

1897   George entered the Virginia Military Institute.   `Age 16`

1902   he became a second lieutenant.
he married Elizabeth Carter "Lily" Coles.   `Age 21`

1917   he became a temporary major.
he began a tour of duty with U.S. forces in
France during World War I.

1919   he became the aide to General John J.
Pershing.

1923   George earned the rank of lieutenant colonel.

1927   he became an instructor for the Army War   `Age 46`
College in Washington, D.C.
his wife, Lily, died.
he became assistant commandant at Infantry
School, Fort Benning, Georgia.

1930   he married Katherine Tupper Brown.

1936   he was promoted to the rank of brigadier   `Age 55`
general.

1939   he became chief of staff of the U.S. Army.

1944   he was promoted to the newly created rank
of five-star general.

1947   he became U.S. secretary of state.   `Age 66`

1949   he became head of the American Red Cross.

1950   he became U.S. secretary of defense.

1953   he received the Nobel Peace Prize for the   `Age 72`
European Recovery Program, also known as
the Marshall Plan.

1959   he died at Walter Reed Army Hospital.   `Age 78`
he was buried in Arlington National
Cemetery.

DUTY ENDS

When Marshall retired, he enjoyed gardening at his home, Dodona Manor in Leesburg, Virginia. Earlier in his life, the garden had been a place to escape the pressures of war.

Marshall did not write a book about his life, as great generals often do. Publishers offered him large amounts of money. But he was afraid what he had to say might hurt too many people. He did let a historian interview him, though.

Marshall didn't have a grand state funeral in the Washington National Cathedral, as many great leaders do. He wanted a simple service at Fort Myer Chapel. He was laid to rest with a simple prayer, "Take Thy servant George."

Marshall's home, Dodona Manor, in Leesburg, Virginia

Further Reading

Barber, Nicola. *World War I: The Western Front.* Mankato, MN: Smart Apple Media, 2003. Discusses the causes of World War I, its main battles, and how the war might have gone differently if different decisions had been made.

Bartlett, Richard. *United States Army.* Chicago: Heinemann Library, 2004. Profiles the U.S. Army, its history, missions, and equipment.

Connolly, Sean. *World War II.* Chicago: Heinemann Library, 2003. Discusses the major causes and events of World War II.

Hughes, Dean. *Soldier Boys.* New York: Atheneum Books for Young Readers, 2001. In this fictional story, two boys, one German and one American, are eager to join their respective armies during World War II, and their paths cross at the Battle of the Bulge.

Websites

The General George C. Marshall International Center at Dodona Manor
http://www.georgecmarshall.org Take a virtual tour of George Marshall's home, Dodona Manor.

George C. Marshall Foundation
http://www.marshallfoundation.org Learn about the George C. Marshall Museum and read more about Marshall's life and career.

Select Bibliography

DeWeerd, Major H. A., ed. *Selected Speeches and Statements of General of the Army George C. Marshall—Chief of Staff United States Army.* Washington, DC: The Infantry Journal, 1945.

Ferrell, Robert H., ed. *The Eisenhower Diaries.* New York: W. W. Norton & Company, 1981.

Marshall, George C. *Memoirs of My Services in the World War, 1917–1918.* Boston: Houghton Mifflin Company, 1976.

Marshall, Katherine Tupper. *Together—Annals of an Army Wife.* New York: Tupper and Love, Inc., 1946.

Pogue, Forrest C. *George C. Marshall: Education of a General, 1880–1939.* New York: Viking Press, 1963.

Pogue, Forrest C. *George C. Marshall: Ordeal and Hope, 1939–1942.* New York: Viking Press, 1966.

Pogue, Forrest C. *George C. Marshall: Organizer of Victory, 1943–1945.* New York: Viking Press, 1973.

Pogue, Forrest C. *George C. Marshall: Statesman, 1945–1959.* New York: Viking Press, 1987.

Wilson, Rose Page. *General Marshall Remembered.* Englewood Cliffs, NJ: Prentice-Hall, 1968.

INDEX

Acknowledgments

For photographs and artwork: Library of Congress, pp. 4, 17, 21, 26; Courtesy of the George C. Marshall Research Library, Lexington, Virginia, pp. 7 (GCMRL #837), 9 (#1514), 13 (#878), 14 (#738), 22 (#230), 24 (#1624), 30 (#1237), 33 (#167), 35 (#1655), 38 (#2507), 39 (#661), 42 (#3067); Illustrated London News, p. 10; © CORBIS, p. 16; National Archives, p. 18, 40; Courtesy of Georgia Archives, p. 23; National Archives, War & Conflict Collection, p. 29; © Michael Nicholson/CORBIS, p. 31; Franklin D. Roosevelt Library, p. 32; Courtesy of Dodona Manor, p. 45. **Front cover:** © Bettmann/ CORBIS. **Back cover:** Courtesy of the George C. Marshall Research Library, Lexington, Virginia. **For quoted material:** p. 6, Leonard Mosley, *Marshall—Hero for Our Times* (New York: Hearst Books, 1982); p. 33, Forrest C. Pogue, *George C. Marshall: Ordeal and Hope, 1939–1942* (New York: Viking Press, 1966); p. 34, Major H. A. DeWeerd, *Selected Speeches and Statements of General of the Army George C. Marshall—Chief of Staff United States Army* (Washington, DC: The Infantry Journal, 1945); p. 45, Forrest C. Pogue, *George C. Marshall: Statesman, 1945–1959* (New York: Viking Press, 1987).